help!

I WANT TO GIVE UP SMOKING

Claire Richardson

SUMMERSDALE

Summersdale Publishers Ltd
46 West Street
Chichester
West Sussex
PO19 1RP
United Kingdom

www.summersdale.com

Printed and bound in Great Britain by Cox & Wyman.

ISBN 1 84024 065 2

Contents

Introduction

The aim of this book is not to shock you with statistics about how bad smoking is for your health. Everyone has their own set of reasons why they started smoking and similarly everybody has a unique collection of reasons to prompt them to think about giving up.

I assume that you have picked up this book because you want to give up. Well, unless you have been living in an isolation tank for the past few decades you cannot help but be aware of the dangers inherent in the common cigarette. Smokers are bombarded by the media, the government, by public opinion day in, day out and their numbers are rapidly decreasing. Smokers are an obstinate and dying breed – literally. But this does not seem to make any difference to those determined to ignore the warnings. 'If three in every ten smokers die of lung cancer, I will definitely be one of the seven who doesn't', you think to yourself, and 'look at Granny, she's smoked for fifty years and she's fit as a fiddle' (sounds familiar?). But you can't bury your head in a cloud of smoke forever.

Hopefully you are reading this book because the niggling feeling that you ought to quit now has got the better of the little devil who says that you can give up any time, and now isn't a good time anyway. Alternatively, perhaps someone who cares about you (or equally detests your habit) is attempting to give you a little nudge in the right direction. But, how often have you been warned that you can only hope to succeed in the battle against the combination of your nicotine addiction and your habit if you are 101% sure that you want to give up?

Unfortunately this is where the 'Catch 22' situation arises. Nobody is ever *certain* that they want to give up smoking. Each person thinking about quitting starts by worrying that they might fail, however this feeling is soon replaced by the all-consuming panic that you might actually SUCCEED. Success at giving up smoking for the smoker is terrifying. You might never smoke another cigarette. Yet you want to quit. This is why giving up smoking can be such a tricky business, if you don't prepare yourself properly.

What this book aims to do is twofold. Firstly, it aims to help you explore the reasons why you smoke, because you are much more likely to be able to give up when you know exactly what it is you are leaving behind when you move into the ranks of the non-smokers. Secondly, it offers practical advice to help you along the path. Yes, it can be done. If you are determined enough you too will soon be entering the ranks of those who say, 'No thanks, I don't smoke.'

I

Why Do You Want To Give Up?

There are a number of reasons why people suddenly decide to give up smoking. The major and most obvious reasons are listed below. As you can see at a glance, the section on health is the shortest, this is by no means because it is the least important, if cigarettes weren't ruining our health we probably wouldn't think twice about giving up. I could devote pages and pages to the numerous smoking-related diseases and the effects that they have on smokers. I could even show you glossy photographs of the inside of smoker's lungs – something to put you off your dinner but probably not your after-dinner cigarette. But, as we know, shock tactics do not work. People who have had limbs amputated through smoking continue to smoke. People who have lost someone close to them from a smoking-related illness continue to smoke. None of these people can possibly ignore the evidence. You can't afford to either.

Reasons why people consider giving up smoking:

Health

Fears for our own health or for those around us, for example children or an asthma-suffering partner. Unborn babies are particularly susceptible because any nicotine absorbed into the mother's bloodstream enters the baby's blood and can cause numerous complications both during and after the birth for both the mother and the baby.

Cost

The rising cost of cigarettes is, bizarrely enough, not usually sufficient a trigger to prompt people into giving up smoking, no matter how dire their financial situation. Smokers have an extraordinary way of justifying their dependence by labelling cigarettes as a 'necessity item' in their minds. Therefore cigarettes are ranked with food, clothes, petrol etc., as a necessity; something that you can't possibly survive without.

The majority of smokers refuse to register that they would be hundreds, possibly even thousands of pounds better off at the end of the year if they did not smoke (imagine what that totals over a fifty year smoking career). Because to a smoker it is like working out how much saving you could make if you didn't eat – a fruitless task! Therefore, the cost alone is rarely a major factor when people give up smoking – although the savings will quickly become apparent.

Social Problems

The increasing social stigma attached to smoking (because everyone is aware of the dangers and they know you know) makes smokers increasingly aware that they are practising a revolting and antisocial habit.

This point was really brought home to me one day when I was having my mid-morning cigarette on the office steps. I was unsuspectingly standing there, unaware that someone might as well have stuck a notice on my forehead that read 'Lecture me, I'm a smoker'. Actually I think the real giveaway was the cigarette drooping from my hand and large clouds of unpleasant-smelling smoke issuing from my mouth. Anyway in the time it had taken me to smoke a cigarette (just under five minutes) I had received two lectures from complete strangers on the dangers of smoking. From that moment on I became increasingly aware of the disapproving looks I received in public places.

Have you noticed people moving away from you in pubs and restaurants? Do children point you out to their parents in the street? Perhaps your own children complain about your habit. Have you ever been asked not to smoke by someone eating near you in a restaurant? Do people comment on the smell when you re-enter the office after a quick puff? If you can answer 'yes' to any of these questions then you will be perfectly aware that smoking is an antisocial habit and a lot of people despise it.

This knowledge may make you more determined than ever not to give up, believing yourself to be exercising your right as a free citizen to smoke. This is a foolhardy approach. You are not going to be doing anyone any favours or proving your point if you go on to develop lung cancer, heart disease, bronchitis or any other of the smoking-related diseases.

Convenience

Smoking is also gradually being forced out of the workplace. Very few smoking offices remain. Increasingly smoking is also banned within the vicinity of the building, so you can't even pop off to the smoking room for a quick fag or loiter on the steps having a puff, instead you have to go and hide behind a bush in the rain. Worse than this, smoking may actually jeopardise your career if you happen to be a sportsman or woman. Just look at the fuss kicked up about Gazza's twenty a day habit and his subsequent removal from the England World Cup team.

Restaurants and public transport are constantly increasing their smoking restrictions. Even the good old British pub, that staid haven of smokiness, is beginning to be affected by the anti-smoking lobby. Therefore simply for the sake of convenience it would actually be far easier not to be a smoker.

Smoking is ruling my life!

How long each day do you spend looking for your cigarettes and lighter and making sure that you always have sufficient quantities on you for the day/ evening/journey? How often have you got dressed again and gone to that late night garage just because you fancy a cigarette and have run out? Have you ever made detours from your route or wandered around aimlessly (and grumpily) attempting to find a newsagent or a bar or anywhere that sells cigarettes?

Wouldn't it be nice not to be late for work simply because you had to buy some fags so that you could have one for your mid-morning coffee break? How many times have you furiously attempted to make that lighter work or scrabbled around for a live match in utter desperation (cursing the person who put all the dead ones back in the box), at the thought that you may be unable to light your cigarette? The panic induced by each of these scenarios, which crop up all the time, increases your daily stress and worry.

Cigarettes govern your life, they are always in the back (if not the front) of your mind, often seeming more important than remembering your car keys or your wallet. Wouldn't it be nice to be free of these shackles and not to have your life ruled by anything as ridiculous as dried up bits of plant soaked in chemicals and rolled up in paper.

At this stage take some time to think about your 'real' reasons for giving up. Write them down starting with what you see to be your most important motivation.

Your list may look something like the following:

- *Health* – Nagging worry and guilt about smoking-related diseases and premature death.
- *Fitness* – I would like to feel generally healthier, not get breathless after minimal exercise.
- *Cost* – I can't afford to smoke and I would rather spend the money I save on a holiday or some new clothes etc.
- *Convenience* – My life would be much easier without cigarettes, I don't want to be a slave to nicotine, always worrying about where my next cigarette is coming from.
- *Taste/smell* – I would like to be able to smell and taste properly again to increase the pleasure that I get from food.
- *Clothing/Furniture* – I don't want my house and clothes to constantly stink of smoke.
- *Partner* – it would save a lot of arguments and unhappiness.
- *I will be a much happier person in myself when I am a non-smoker.*

Keep this list safe and add to it as you think of more reasons why your life would be better without cigarettes. It will come in very handy later.

2

Why Do You Smoke?

Habit and Addiction

Considering the fact that most smokers in their heart of hearts would like to give up there must be other factors at work preventing these people giving up smoking. These factors are *habit* and *addiction*.

Various 'experts' on giving up the weed have attempted to divide up the amount of physical addiction and mental dependence on smoking. Some believe that reliance on cigarettes is mainly in the mind, others state that it is actually in the brain (i.e. their body's addiction to the nicotine in tobacco).

Unfortunately, the study of giving up smoking is not an exact science, therefore no one can say for definite that quitting is 10% mental and 90% physical or vice versa. However, we can be sure that both *addiction* and *habit* are responsible for our reliance on cigarettes. Although it is extremely difficult to separate these two causes – because the human being is a complex creature and there is a fine line between MIND and BRAIN in our understanding – it is helpful to go some way towards identifying the reasons why we continue to smoke, knowing that the odds are stacked against us. Therefore in order to try and understand why we smoke and thus give up, we have to be able to examine these two issues separately.

Addiction

Your addiction to nicotine is the thing that sustains your 'habit'. You would never have become a regular smoker if nicotine were not a drug that is as addictive as heroin (and one that claims far more lives than the Class A drug).

Most people dislike their first ever cigarette. The taste is unpleasant and may make you cough and splutter; after all the human body is not designed to inhale quantities of tar and numerous other poisonous chemicals in gaseous form.

Perhaps you can remember your first cigarette (before your body adapted to the nicotine) or maybe you have heard your non-smoking friends saying that they tried one once and didn't enjoy it. These were the lucky ones, the people who listened to their body's signals. However, due to pressure or image, a large number of people persist to try another one – after all, so many people do it, there must be something going for smoking – and another.

Unfortunately, within about three days your body becomes adapted to your recreational drug of choice, nicotine, and begins to crave another fix. When this craving is satisfied, your body believes it is experiencing 'pleasure' – because satisfying a craving results in a pleasurable feeling. This is where the myth that you actually 'enjoy' smoking comes from. This is not genuine pleasure, like that derived from receiving an unexpected present or spending a night out with friends, it is a purely chemical reaction to topping up your nicotine levels. Therefore your addiction to nicotine is actually conning you into thinking that you would miss smoking because you enjoy it so much.

Habit

A habit is 'an action or practice which has become automatic through repetition'. How many times have you lit a cigarette without really thinking about it? Have you ever lit a cigarette whilst you still have one smoking in the ashtray? This is automation. You are not really thinking about what you are doing and often your body is not actually craving nicotine (especially if you are chain smoking). Your habit or dependence is in your mind, however we cannot simply make up our minds to do something about it because it is combined with the addictive effects of nicotine.

If you think about it there is probably a definite pattern to the cigarettes that you smoke during an average day. Write down a list of the cigarettes that you invariably smoke during the day, starting with the first one of the morning and ending with your last one at night – detailing at roughly what time you smoke them and what you are doing at the time. Below is the sample list of a 10-15 a day smoker – obviously if you are a heavier smoker your day will be punctuated by more cigarette breaks.

- 8.30am   – 1 in the car on the way to work
- 10.30am   – 1 mid-morning with a coffee
- 12.30-1.30pm – 2 at lunchtime
- 4.00pm   – 1 mid-afternoon
- 5.30pm   – 1 on your journey home
- 6.30-8.00pm – 1-2 relaxing when you get home
- 9.00pm   – 1 after supper
- 9.30-11.30pm – 1-2 before bed

This list does *not* include the evenings that you might go out or variations that occur at the weekend. You will probably also smoke others in between these, depending on what you are doing. Nevertheless your list forms the structure of your habit and will come in useful at a later stage, because you will be alert to the danger times when you are most likely to crave a cigarette.

By studying your list and the timings of your 'usual' cigarettes you will probably notice that the gaps between them are roughly even (in this case approximately 1½ hours). This illustrates the close connection between your habit and your addiction:

your addiction to nicotine governs when you need your next fix and turns it into a daily routine or habit. It is the combination of habit and addiction that causes cigarettes to rule our lives.

Although your addiction to nicotine has to be overcome, fortunately habits are designed to be changed rather than broken. Although the excuse that 'I can't give up, it's a habit', is often used by smokers, it is not a valid one. Simply because for those of us without obsessive/compulsive disorders habits do not rule our lives.

However, it must be stressed here that without an addiction, smoking would never have become the problem that it is to you now. In that respect the addiction outweighs the habit and it is actually misleading and unhelpful to refer to smoking purely as a habit. You might be in the habit of drinking a cup of cocoa before you go to bed, going swimming twice a week or brushing your teeth at bedtime. All these activities may be described as habits, however if you couldn't have/do one of them on a particular day, it might ruin your routine, but it will not have anything like the same effect upon you as not being able to have a cigarette. Therefore to classify smoking as a habit implies that, like a game of squash on a Friday evening, it is easy to forego. As we know, this is not the case.

3

Smokers From The Outsider's Perspective

Take a step back from being a smoker and open your mind. Imagine that you come from a civilised society similar to ours but you have never seen anyone smoking. You are aware of the health problems that are caused by air pollution from industry and transport, but this is something else!

What this peculiar society is doing for 'pleasure' is absolutely extraordinary! In a society where pioneering research into new medicines and longevity is being undertaken every day – where constant attempts are being made by the government to improve the health service – a large proportion of the population appear to be undermining this progress. In fact they are rather like lemmings with a death wish, herding together to plummet off a cliff. Stranger still, the very same government that is putting so much money into health care (a considerable proportion of which is spent on combating smoking-related diseases), is benefiting enormously from the extortionate tax on the sale of this product!

Probably the most bizarre aspect of this mass 'smoking' phenomenon is the fact that the people doing it look so utterly ridiculous. These 'cigarettes', the cause of all the problems, are rolled up pieces of paper packed with dried leaves and soaked in toxic chemicals. This construction is then lit at one end and the 'smoker' inhales the noxious fumes into their lungs (yes, they are actually filling their lungs with a poisonous gaseous concoction of over 4,000 chemicals, including tar and nicotine, which is almost guaranteed to cause them health problems in later life). The smoke is then exhaled through the nose and the mouth in a particularly unpleasant fashion that causes coughing, sore throats and eye irritations in the short term and far worse complications in the long term. Strangely enough everyone is perfectly aware of the risks but does not seem to be doing anything about it.

This is the sort of behaviour that you might attribute to some isolated tribe who are unaware of the health risks – surely not to a developed, well-informed, educated population such as this? How wrong can you be?

The burning question remains, why do almost 13 million people in the UK alone keep on smoking despite the risks? These people are not stupid, ignorant people who don't realise that they are killing themselves. The majority are perfectly intelligent individuals who are quite aware of the risks that they are taking – yet they persist in lighting up day in day out.

4

What Is Preventing You Giving Up?

There are numerous excuses that people use for the 'benefit' of themselves and others, as to why they should not give up smoking. However these are not simply reasons that smokers make up off the top of their heads to excuse their habit, they actually believe them. Nicotine has fooled these people (and you may be one of them) into coming up with reasons to continue smoking, which to the majority of non-smokers probably sound absurd. I am not saying that you, the smoker, are being stupid, smoking is simply like being tricked by a con man. However, like the con man, once you have either been fooled once or been warned about the tactics he uses you are unlikely to make the same mistake again.

Therefore in order to get the better of nicotine you have to be aware of the traps that it puts in your path and the many guises it can adopt. By examining these you will learn to outwit nicotine and prevent it from surprising you.

Below are listed some of the typical worries experienced by people toying with the idea that they ought to give up smoking. There are always plenty of reasons why you *shouldn't* give up smoking. However, as we shall see most of these 'reasons' are myths, the fruit of a manipulative substance called 'nicotine', that can make even the most level-headed person come up with the most ridiculous justification as to why they could and should not give up smoking. These are some of the most common ones:

- **'Smoking stops me feeling empty'**

   The main problem lies in the fact that the majority of people started smoking when they were adolescents or teenagers (few people start smoking in their twenties or later). This is typically a period of confusion and discovery, people are often depressed, lonely and mixed up. At that age you were probably looking to fill what was seen as a void in your life; a hole which you believed should have been occupied by friends or a boyfriend or girlfriend. Cigarettes were seen as a means of plugging this gap.

   Adolescents are also desperate to 'fit in' to be part of the gang, to be liked and admired. Smoking is seen as a way to both fill the void and give us credibility with our peers. Smoking also has the added bonus of being rebellious and challenging the authority of our parents, teachers etc.

   You probably still see smoking as filling a gap in your life, consequently, without it there would be something missing and you would feel empty and depressed again.

• *'Smoking helps me cope when life is hard'*

If you begin smoking during a particularly traumatic period of your life, you start to believe that the cigarettes themselves have helped you to get through this particularly difficult time and emerge the other side in one piece. For example you may have lost someone close to you, lost your job or split up with a partner. Any number of difficult situations see people reaching for nicotine, because they think that they can't cope on their own. You see cigarettes as your support, without which you will not be able to face the day.

• *'I enjoy smoking too much'*

This is one of the frequent responses to the question: 'Why don't you give up smoking?' You think that smoking is a pleasurable activity and without it you would not gain so much enjoyment out of life. You think that you would feel constantly deprived, that cigarettes are your friends – without them you would feel a sense of loss.

- **'I won't be able to cope with the pressures of daily life without a cigarette'**

  Perhaps you have a stressful job or you are a full-time parent – equally exhausting, if not more so – and you don't have much opportunity to relax and unwind. You probably see smoking as a regular five minutes when you can clear your head, relieve your stress and then tackle the next problem. Your stress levels might become unmanageable if you were to give up smoking; how would you let off steam?

- **'Smoking helps me concentrate. I would not operate so well without cigarettes'**

  Maybe when you are really craving a cigarette you begin to find it difficult to concentrate. Do you find it hard to think clearly and get increasingly fidgety? Smoking a cigarette seems to focus your mind and helps you to focus on the task in hand. How then will you be able to keep your head at work or concentrate at home if you no longer smoke?

- **'I won't know what to do with my hands if I give up'**

Like an actor who needs stage props to support their performance, the smoker has over the years leant on their habit for support. You may have been smoking ever since you have been allowed (or not as the case may be) in pubs and bars. The thought of being unable to socialise with a beer in one hand and a fag in the other may send paroxysms of fear through you.

- **'Smoking makes me feel confident'**

You have probably been smoking since an age when you were not so confident, when you were more worried what people thought of you and whether you 'fitted in' than you are now. However, even now, when you are feeling uncertain of yourself you can light a cigarette and worries will disappear – things will be all right.

- **'I'll be bored if I don't smoke'**

Perhaps smoking keeps you occupied at times when you don't have anything to do. It stops you being bored by keeping your mind and your hands busy. You think that you would probably get bored and find that you did not have enough to do if you weren't a smoker.

- **'I won't know what to do when I have a few minutes to kill'**

Perhaps smoking occupies you whilst waiting for somebody or when you are killing time. What will you do in that five minutes while you are waiting for the train if you don't smoke? You will stand around looking like a fish out of water and everybody will wonder why you are doing nothing. Ah, but if you are smoking you are doing something!

- **'All my friends smoke'**

How could you possibly be expected to give up when all your friends smoke – it would be impossible, they would keep offering you cigarettes and sooner or later the temptation would become too great. Besides you enjoy being part of the crowd and having a social cigarette or twenty!

- **'I won't be able to give up'**

  Maybe you are generally successful in most spheres of your life and don't want to be seen as a failure. On the other hand perhaps you just don't trust yourself or think you have the will power to kick the habit for good, so it's probably not worth you wasting your energy anyway.

- **'What do I do if I actually manage to give up?'**

  What happens if even after your other worries and excuses, you actually manage to give up smoking. You will never be able to have another cigarette. You will be deprived of this pleasure for the rest of your life. PANIC. No, nothing could be worse than actually succeeding in the quest to give up smoking.

- **'I often smoke when I'm hungry, I'll put on weight if I give up'**

  When you get hungry you have a cigarette (this is particularly true of women I am afraid) and it stops you feeling hungry, prevents you snacking on that bar of chocolate or that packet of crisps. If you give up you might put on weight and then you wouldn't be happy with your appearance any more, so you'd rather remain a smoker.

• *'I smoke because I can – it's my right and my body!'*

You may believe that you smoke because you can, because you are a free citizen and although the government can exercise controls in public places, in the privacy of your own home or the great outdoors you can smoke – it's not illegal after all, is it.

From the above it would seem that cigarettes are a wonder drug. Doesn't it seem amazing that a few tobacco leaves lit and inhaled at regular intervals can improve all aspects of your social life, working life, appearance, emotional stability, occupy your mind and your spare time, help you concentrate and think more clearly. Unfortunately you know in your heart of hearts that this is not the case and that you are just fooling yourself, or more to the point, the nicotine is fooling you!

5

Destroying The Myths

Although you may think that smoking is a very personal thing to you, and that coffee break would not be as relaxing, that sunset as beautiful or that meal so enjoyable had you not been able to smoke – smokers fall into surprisingly similar patterns (as you can probably recognise from Chapter 4). It is because of this that it is possible to identify the trouble spots in your life, the areas that you need to alter if you are to successfully give up smoking, and by doing so make facing the inevitable considerably easier when it actually happens.

In order to give up smoking we must examine each individual worry, destroy the myth surrounding it and suggest how to approach and tackle them as they arise. Although some situations can initially be totally avoided, thereby removing the temptation – unfortunately this is not the case in all scenarios. In these cases you will need to be totally aware of the risk of temptation and simply be strong-willed about not letting it get the better of you. Recognising these 'danger' areas means that you will be prepared to do battle with the nicotine monster.

You also need to go some way towards figuring out why you smoke in order to prepare yourself before you can begin to attempt to kick the habit – and more importantly, the addiction – so read on.

- *'Smoking stops me feeling empty'*

– **Destroying the Myth**

The problem lies in the fact that this 'void' never really existed, or needed to be filled, it is simply a necessary period in each person's development. Cigarettes are seen as a means to fill this emptiness. Unfortunately as we get older we remain convinced that there is a void in our lives that needs to be filled by tobacco. In fact this is a self-perpetuating myth – it is actually nicotine deprivation that creates the feelings of restlessness, stress, lack of confidence and generally a need for something – which manifests itself as a need for nicotine.

Look at all those people who never started smoking; they don't see their lives as lacking something, they don't feel lonely or restless without smoking. Nicotine itself created the void that it goes on to fulfil, in just another vicious circle. For smokers this desire identifies itself simply in the 'need' for a cigarette. How often have you heard or uttered 'I need a cigarette' or 'I'm desperate for a fag' or even 'I'd kill for a cigarette right now'?

• *'Smoking helps me cope when life is hard'*

– *Destroying the Myth*

The truth is that you would have got through that rocky period of your life without smoking and you will be able to face the obstacles that life has a habit of scattering in your path again if you give up smoking. It is simply that your mind equates difficult times with dependence on cigarettes. Smoking merely provides an imaginary crutch, which when removed means that you can function just as effectively if not more so. All the time you believe that cigarettes are helping you, they are in fact hindering you considerably and preventing you from leading a happier and healthier lifestyle.

You think that you need cigarettes, you think that your life would be much worse and far less enjoyable without them – but this is all part of the nicotine trick. When you give up you will soon realise that all this time cigarettes have simply been slowing you down and preventing you reaching your true potential. You can do it on your own, you can't hide behind a packet of cigarettes and a collection of feeble excuses forever; sooner or later you will have to take responsibility for your own life.

• *'I enjoy smoking too much'*

– *Destroying the Myth*

We already know that the actual 'pleasure' and enjoyment derived from smoking a cigarette is illusory and merely the nicotine trying to trick us, however, the trap is more cunning than that. The reason for this is that not only is a smoker satisfying a craving every time they light a cigarette, resulting in a feeling of pleasure, but people also tend to smoke a lot in social situations, where others are smoking. This socialising usually take place with friends – therefore cigarettes quickly become associated with having a good time. The fact that you are enjoying yourself has nothing to do with the fact that you are smoking and everything to do with the fact that you are out with people whose company you enjoy.

Most smokers freely admit that they do not enjoy every cigarette they light and the ones who say they do are probably lying. You won't have to think too hard to name the cigarettes that you generally enjoy the most, it is likely that they include some, if not all, of those listed below:

- Relaxing with a cup of coffee/tea.

- After a large meal.

- After work with a cold beer.

- After stressful activity, for example a weekly shopping trip/ getting the kids to bed.

- On a particularly beautiful summer evening...

You probably rarely enjoy the first cigarette of the day and it is most likely that you get little 'pleasure' from 50% if not more of the cigarettes that you smoke during an average day. In fact you are not enjoying over half the money that you are burning!

If you don't believe me, keep a daily diary of every cigarette that you smoke for a week and rate them from 1–5 on a basis of the enjoyment/ pleasure that you gained from them (1 = 'not at all' and 5 = 'a great deal'). You will have to be really honest with yourself, because if you can't be there is little chance of you actually giving up smoking. At the end of the week work out exactly how many of the cigarettes you smoked scored a 4 or more on the enjoyment scale and compare that figure with the total number you have smoked.

• *'I won't be able to cope with the pressures of daily life without a cigarette'*

– Destroying the Myth

This is another nicotine trap to keep you smoking. Although you believe that cigarettes remove stress, they in fact create the feelings of stress: due to withdrawal from your last cigarette. You think that you have had a particularly stressful morning and that your lunchtime cigarette has eased way all that tension so that you can return to your job and face the afternoon. In fact what has actually happened is that although something may have happened to increase your stress levels, these are being heightened by nicotine deprivation. This leads to the vicious circle of:

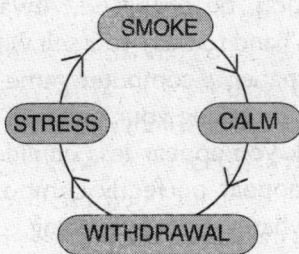

```
           SMOKE
          ↗      ↘
    STRESS        CALM
          ↖      ↙
         WITHDRAWAL
```

How do you suppose that all those non-smokers and reformed smokers manage to get through their day without falling apart?

• *'Smoking makes me feel confident'*

– Destroying the Myth

Cigarettes are a confidence trick! Smoking has been glamorised by cigarette advertisers and the media. You probably also think that you look and feel more confident smoking a cigarette. But would you actually turn into a nervous wreck if you could no longer, through choice, use cigarettes as a prop? Would you think any less of someone waiting for a friend or merely sitting alone, reading a newspaper or simply staring into space? In fact these people exude more confidence because they are not reliant on tobacco as a crutch.

If you are nervous about finding yourself in this sort of situation, be prepared. Always have something on hand to busy yourself with, like a book, a newspaper, a computer game or even your knitting. By taking your mind off the fact that you think you appear less confident, you will actually appear perfectly composed and absorbed in whatever you are doing.

• *'I'll be bored if I don't smoke'*

– Destroying the Myth

I remember a rather irritating saying that my mother used to repeat to me when I was younger: 'Only boring people get bored'. Although it used to infuriate me at the time I can see now that there is probably a grain of truth in this old wives tale. It is all a question of motivation, there is always something that you can be doing, even if it is simply something like going for a walk or cleaning the cooker, it will occupy your time and your mind.

A common myth is that smoking relieves boredom, probably issuing from the time when you first started smoking and you used to hang around with your mates killing time instead of doing something fun or constructive. In fact smoking promotes boredom. Instead of doing something constructive when you have got a few spare minutes you simply kill time by smoking. You light a cigarette to prevent yourself actually having to do anything else. Anyway, the feeling that you identify as 'boredom' is actually more likely to be the restless, empty feeling symptomatic of nicotine withdrawal from your last cigarette. Therefore without the cigarette in the first instance you would not experience this feeling.

• *'I won't know what to do when I have a few minutes to kill'*

– *Destroying the Myth*

This problem will probably not even arise because the chances are that you hurried to the station, so as to make sure that you had time for that last cigarette before you boarded your non-smoking train. A great majority of the time smokers specifically engineer situations so that they can have a quick puff. If you are no longer a smoker you will not create these scenarios and the problem will not arise in the first place. If you do find yourself hanging about at a loose end, find something to occupy you. Browse in a nearby shop (not a tobacconist), buy a paper or simply people-watch to take your mind off smoking. After all non-smokers don't have this problem, do they.

- *'All my friends smoke'*

- **Destroying the Myth**

For most people this is probably an exaggeration. Smokers form a minority of the population and people increasingly give up as they get older and realise that they are no longer indestructible. Make a list of your friends, acquaintances and people that you spend time with. Then label them smokers or non-smokers (ex-smokers fall into the latter category). You will most probably find that you know just as many people who don't smoke as those who do. This will ring truer the older you are (because as I have already said, people tend to start smoking when they are young to be 'part of the gang' therefore it is fairly likely that they will congregate with smokers). If all your friends really do smoke then giving up is bound to be a little more difficult – but you can do it.

As long as you don't become a parsimonious ex-smoker everything will be fine. Your friends may have always known you as a smoker, but it is not an identity tag. If you suddenly started drinking gin & tonic instead of lager, it may take them a little while to get used to it and they may buy you a lager by mistake occasionally, however if they are real friends their views about you will not have changed! The same is true of cigarettes. You are the same person, you just don't have smoke exuding from your nose and mouth at regular intervals. They may try to offer you a cigarette but you must remember that they are merely trying to ease their own conscience, so don't give in and compromise your feelings in the process.

Admittedly any situation that involves alcohol and a smoky atmosphere such as a pub, bar or club is going to be a challenge simply due to the years of association between a pint and a fag. These sorts of situations are definitely to be avoided – at least for the first week or so after giving up – as alcohol weakens your resolve. As a result you may convince yourself that you can just have one or two or a whole packet and before you have time to say 'Mine's a pint' you'll be a fully-fledged smoker again.

I am not advocating that you sabotage your social life, just be sensible, know your limits and don't put unnecessary temptation in your path. If you are still desperate to do something with your hands buy a set of worry beads and play with them (destroying beer mats and lighting endless matches is guaranteed to irritate and is a telltale sign of someone who is attempting to give up smoking).

- *'I won't be able to give up'*
- *'What if I actually manage to give up?'*

– Destroying the Myths

These two statements may appear to contradict one another, but they don't. Fear is the main emotion preventing smokers from giving up. Perhaps you are a generally successful person in all areas of your life, but your one weakness is smoking. You may think that you will be labelled a failure if you don't succeed and use this as an excuse for not even bothering to try. However, with typical smoker's logic, the fear that you might succeed actually outweighs the fear that you might not.

Imagine never being able to smoke another cigarette again. Does this bring you out in a cold sweat? Everybody can physically give up smoking, but it is precisely this knowledge that is hindering them. However this fear is irrational, non-smokers and ex-smokers are just as capable, probably more so, of coping with life, because they do not have to rely on a prop. They can get through the day without resorting to a drug. Therefore they do not become unnecessarily stressed about not having their next fix of nicotine.

- *'I often smoke when I'm hungry, I'll put on weight if I give up'*

– Destroying the Myth

A lot of people (especially women) worry about putting on weight when they give up smoking. In fact a great number of teenage girls take up smoking precisely because cigarettes act as an appetite suppressant. However if you prepare yourself and your fridge for giving up you can minimise immediate weight gain. Remember, even if you do put on a small amount of weight to begin with, careful eating combined with exercise will make you feel a lot healthier than you did when you were a smoker.

- *'I smoke because I can – it's my right and my body'*

– Destroying the Myth

One of the excuses that people use to not give up smoking and to continue to blow smoke in the face of governmental, medical and media persecution is that they believe they are exercising the right of free citizens to smoke. Therefore no matter how much duty the Chancellor of the Exchequer puts on cigarettes this year or how many new diseases are linked to smoking people will still smoke. Even though it is damaging your health and your finances, you still smoke. Why? Simply because you can, you think to yourself. Smokers are all in the same boat, which is looking increasingly like the Titanic.

Smokers give complete strangers a light, they congregate in the rain outside non-smoking offices, they sneak off together from meals in non-smoking restaurants and offer their cigarettes around at parties. Being a smoker is like being part of a great universal club. Unfortunately, the only requirement for membership is the inability to take control of your own life and quit smoking.

How many times have your friends, colleagues, work mates offered you a cigarette when you are attempting to give up? (Or perhaps you have done it to them!) Why is this? An individual is making a positive effort to give up smoking and they are attempting to sabotage it. This is simply because they feel guilty. They fear that you may have seen the light and are thinking about leaving the gang. Who will they go for their mid-morning cigarette break with now?

Unfortunately although smokers believe that they are free, the only thing really uniting them is their complete lack of freedom of action. They are not resisting the attempts of the authorities to make them stop, they are simply unable to resist the temptation of another cigarette. Don't kid yourself.

6

Facing Your Enemies; Habit and Addiction

Many doctors and experts dealing with giving up smoking advocate the 'cold turkey' approach – unfortunately this often means stop today and face the consequences as they happen. Unfortunately this approach is doomed to failure for most. You must be both mentally and physically prepared when the time comes for you to give up. By considering the problems before they confront you, you can be ready with the correct course of action. Be prepared – rather than quitting first and thinking later – because your ability to be rational when suffering withdrawal symptoms from nicotine is severely limited. To those who are unprepared the problems faced when giving up smoking will appear far greater than the initial problem of actually being a smoker. It is these people who are most likely to fail.

Therefore, if you have a good idea of the problems that are going to face you and how to overcome them when you do, you will have a much higher chance of success. The former method is similar to going into battle without a strategy and not knowing who or where your enemies are. How can you hope to outwit them? However with detailed intelligence reports you can outsmart the enemy (in this case nicotine) before it kills you.

Confronting Your Habit

Look back at the list of your habitual daily cigarettes that you made in Chapter 4. These times are your 'danger times'. It is at these times, like your journey to work or your lunch break that you will have to plan alternatives to keep you busy.

Example 1 – Driving to Work

Although you can't safely 'do' anything else when you are driving, make sure that you *don't* have any cigarettes in the car and *do* have a supply of mints or chewing gum handy. You could take some soothing music to listen to or alternatively something to sing along to, to keep your mind busy.

Example 2 – Lunch Break

Break your usual routine. If you normally go to lunch with a smoking friend or colleague, change your pattern (you will probably have to explain, so that they don't take offence). Take a sandwich to the park and read a book instead. As soon as you begin to feel 'restless' go and browse in the shops or buy those little things that you have meant to purchase for ages.

Example 3 – After a Meal

This is a difficult cigarette to forgo, because you are generally sitting about and you may also have company. The answer to this danger time is not to sit around and torture yourself. Instead, get up and clear the table, or go and do the washing up. Sounds dull I know, but it will prevent you from smoking.

This may be more difficult if you are in a restaurant. If you are in the company of smokers, sit near non-smokers and if the urge to smoke gets too strong, simply get up and go outside for a breath of fresh air to clear your head.

Obviously these are just examples and your own smoking pattern may look totally different to this. Refer to your individual smoking diary again and devise an alternative 'game plan' to simply having a cigarette for each 'danger time'. By doing this you will be prepared in your mind for each situation as it occurs.

Confronting Your Addiction – Withdrawal Symptoms

The main withdrawal 'symptom' from nicotine, or the one you are most likely to recognise is also the most obvious: the overwhelming desire to have a cigarette, which is the reason why people find it so hard to give up. Despite the fact that withdrawal generally manifests itself in the thought: 'I need a cigarette', there are a number of different emotions and physical symptoms that comprise this desire for a cigarette. By looking at the physical withdrawal symptoms of nicotine separately, it is easier to break down this urge to smoke into something more comprehensible and easier to overcome.

The problems faced when withdrawing physically from a drug are much more scientific and easier to quantify than those faced when attempting to overcome your psychological dependence, although they do vary slightly from person to person. Nevertheless, estimates for the period that these withdrawal symptoms from smoking actually last ranges from about 3 days to about 3 weeks. Despite this discrepancy we are aware that:

- Actual physical withdrawal from nicotine lasts less than a month and may actually be experienced for a much shorter period depending on the individual (no matter how long you have smoked for or how many you smoke a day).

• After that period you are no longer addicted to cigarettes, therefore what you may think are withdrawal symptoms after this period are caused either by your body convalescing or your psychological dependence.

• Withdrawal symptoms are usually physically mild and may include:

    – Headaches
    – Coughing
    – Hunger pangs/ cravings for sweet substances
    – Stress
    – Irritability
    – Inability to concentrate / restlessness
    – Tiredness
    – Stomach/intestinal problems
    – Sleep disturbance

The withdrawal period is when your body is ridding itself of remaining nicotine deposits, so that the addiction can no longer be sustained. After this any unusual symptoms that you develop, such as coughing, are probably a result of your body attempting to recover from years of abuse. Suddenly your *cilia*, the tiny hairs that are designed to clear out your lungs, can work again because they are no longer being bombarded by tar. As a result, all the tar that has been clogging up your poor lungs is loosened and you slowly begin to cough it up. You may have been under the false impression that simply because you did not have a smoker's cough when you did smoke, you weren't doing yourself any real harm. Not true! It is actually better for you to cough in order to rid the toxins from your lungs, if you don't they simply build up and do even more damage.

'I feel worse, so what's the point!'

When you reach this stage you may think that you actually felt healthier when you were a smoker, and seeing as the whole point of giving up in the first place was probably to feel healthier, you might be tempted to take it up again. Don't! This is far from the truth, your lungs will make a speedy recovery, with most ex-smokers returning to the state that their non-smoking compatriots are at within about seven years. Look upon this short period of withdrawal as one of convalescence, where your body is ridding itself of the toxins that have clogging it up for so long.

Dealing with the Physical Withdrawal Symptoms

Hunger Pangs

The reasons why smoking is associated with hunger and weight gain are that:

- Smoking dampens hunger, so instead of eating many smokers have a cigarette. Smoking satisfies this hunger pang temporarily.

- The body's metabolic rate slows down slightly after you give up smoking.

- Nicotine increases our blood sugar level. The withdrawal from nicotine causes a drop in those levels, which in turn increases the body's craving for sweet substances.

- Often the desire to smoke is mistaken for hunger.

Although stopping smoking doesn't necessarily lead to weight gain, unfortunately, many people who give up smoking compensate by eating more – usually sweet and fattening – food. Therefore, especially for those people conscious of their weight it is best to be prepared for this withdrawal symptom. If you are not, the likelihood is that you will think that the only way to lose the weight that you have gained is to take up smoking again, which would be a grave mistake.

Instead if you must succumb to your hunger or need to fill that 'empty space' left by nicotine, try and eat three regular meals, as well as having a supply of healthy low-fat options available to you at all times. These include:

- fruit
- vegetables, e.g. carrots and celery sticks
- high energy, low fat foods like pasta, rice and potatoes
- replace chocolate or sweets with a cereal bar or low-fat alternative

Don't be tempted to snack on . . .

- chocolate
- dairy products
- biscuits

… unless you are not that bothered about possible weight gain. The best way to remain trim and healthy is to combine thoughtful eating with exercise of some description (see below).

Stress

The best way to deal with stress is to remove the object of your anxiety, however this is not always possible. If your stress is caused by a build-up of minor 'stressors', the best thing you can do is to deal with them one by one in a logical manner, rather than putting them all off until tomorrow and have them hanging over you like a black cloud.

Before you actually give up smoking, write yourself a list starting with the minor stresses in your life and working down to the more fundamental problems. Attempt to tackle as many of these problems as you can before you give up, so that when you are experiencing the 'stress' of nicotine withdrawal you are not simultaneously attempting to deal with all the other problems that you having been hoping will magically disappear.

In order to combat stress, especially if you are particularly prone to it, teach yourself some deep breathing exercises to calm yourself down and practise them prior to giving up. If you suffer badly from stress, research into local yoga or relaxation courses and enrol prior to the big day.

Deep Breathing

This simple deep-breathing exercise can be done just about anywhere and will help you to relax. Use it when you feel that the stress is becoming to much for you:

1. Sit comfortably with your feet on the floor.

2. Close your eyes, relax your shoulders and your jaw muscles.

3. Slowly breathe in through your nose, hold your breath in and count to five.

4. Then slowly let your breath out.

Repeat this exercise as often as you feel that you need to.

Irritability

This is possibly one of the most difficult withdrawal symptoms to combat because it may result in bad moods and depression. You probably will experience mood swings especially in the first few days when your body is really suffering from nicotine withdrawal. The thing to bear in mind at all times is that this will only last for a matter of days.

When you find yourself being unreasonable, take a deep breath and a step back from a situation that you may be blowing out of all proportion. Always remember that irritability is a minor side effect of giving up, which in the long term will make your life much more pleasant, and more importantly longer. Warn those close to you at home and work that you will probably be a pain for a couple of days, because you are giving up. They will undoubtedly make allowances for you because you are trying to give up a highly addictive and damaging drug, and everyone is aware of the difficulties.

Restlessness/fidgetiness/boredom

If you experience any of these emotions, go and do something. Go for a walk to clear your mind. Instead of popping out for that five-minute cigarette break, go for a brisk walk around the block.

The best way to combat these withdrawal symptoms is through physical activity. Another vital part of the quitting process is making sure that you're really feeling the benefits, so that you are aware of the improvement in your health and are not tempted to start again. Exercise is one way of both preventing you feeling restless and fidgety, as well as occupying your time well and helping you to feel better about the benefits of the new non-smoking you.

Exercise

If you do not take regular exercise, take up a 'sport' of some sort. Although to the couch potatoes amongst us, this may conjure up exhausting images of sweating on a running machine or getting laid into on a muddy, cold rugby pitch – exercise can be fun. Here are some suggestions:

Sports Centres

Check out the courses at your local sports centre. You can usually try anything from yoga, aerobics to aqua aerobics (from beginners to advanced). These are fun ways to keep fit, use up your nervous energy, make you feel better about yourself and help you appreciate the new fitter, healthier, non-smoking model of your former self.

Swimming

Go swimming at your local pool. This is refreshing after a day at work and great entertainment for the children and is good for toning the muscles without causing you to break out in a sweat, become red in the face and gasp for breath.

Cycling

Get your rusty old bicycle out of the garage, pump up the tyres and take up cycling. Perhaps you live close enough to your workplace to cycle. This not only saves petrol money, but is also fantastic exercise with a purpose, for those who see gyms as a pointless waste of effort – killing two birds with one stone.

Racket Sports

Take tennis or squash lessons. Polish up your existing skills or join an adult beginners class. This is also a great way of meeting like-minded people and making new friends.

Other Alternatives

If all this still sounds too much like hard work, simply take up walking. Go for a brisk stroll. Walk to the corner shop instead of driving etc. For other helpful ideas about how to get fit you could also read *Help! I Want To Get Fit*, packed with helpful hints and tips for those who want to improve their fitness with minimal effort, which is also part of this series.

Tiredness

You may feel much more tired than usual when you are giving up smoking. If you are able, it may be best to go with these feelings and take more rest until you regain your energy. At least when you are asleep, you won't be thinking about smoking!

Nicotine Substitutes?

It is probably best to deal with your withdrawal all at once. It may make you feel bad but you know that this feeling is attributable to the removal of nicotine from your body. Nicotine substitutes replace the nicotine, killing the craving. Therefore, in theory, you can deal with your habit and addiction separately.

Unfortunately, people can become reliant on the nicotine in patches, chewing gum or inhalators. Although nicotine substitutes do not contain the dangers inherent in the common cigarette (it is the tar and other chemicals in tobacco that are so bad for our health), because you have not removed the nicotine addiction it is easy to start smoking again – which is dangerous if you are using nicotine substitutes. If this is your first attempt to quit, go it alone!

However, if you have made numerous failed attempts at giving up, nicotine substitutes may give you the added confidence you need to give up. Follow the instructions carefully and do not exceed the prescribed dose (never smoke at the same time). Seek advice from your doctor or chemist on when to cut down and eventually stop using the substitutes. Remember: you are now going to have to wean yourself off these as well!

7

Extra Motivational Tips

If you need a little extra motivation, other than the promise of improved health (and to be honest don't we all), try one of these tried and tested methods of helping you to give up smoking.

- Give up with a friend. Both put a reasonable sum of money in a pot and agree that if EITHER of you smoke you will give the whole lot to charity. This means that you will encourage each other because you have nothing to gain from your friend smoking and plenty to lose (including a friend!) if you fail.

- Tell everyone you know that you are giving up and that even if in a fit of desperation you get down on your knees in public and beg them for a cigarette, not to succumb.

- Add up how much you spend a week on cigarettes and save it in a jar (if you are a fifty a day smoker you might have to set up a direct debit into a savings account!). After a smoke-free six months treat yourself to something really nice. You can probably afford a holiday or a new stereo.

- Add up how much you spend a month on smoking and spend it instead on joining the local sports or health club, so you can combine giving up smoking with really feeling the benefits of your new healthier lifestyle.

• A really nasty one is to put half an inch of water in the bottom of a jar and add the contents of one particularly foul ashtray. Put the lid on the jar. When you are having a really bad craving for a cigarette, open the jar and take a sniff. That should be enough to put you off for a while!

You have probably heard of many other similar ideas. Tailor the above to suit you, so that you feel you are really getting something positive out of giving up, rather than being left with the negative, empty feeling of not smoking. Incentives really *do* work, they are part of human nature – people don't mind making sacrifices so much if they know that they are getting something good in return.

8

Giving Up Smoking

I realise that I have spent a considerable part of this book theorising with 'ifs' and 'buts' and you may well be thinking 'when is she going to stop rambling on and get to the point?' If you are thinking this then unfortunately you have missed the point of this book and you had better go back and read the first seven chapters again.

What I have been attempting to do is to highlight the worries that people have about giving up smoking, as well as how they can combat both these and the physical withdrawal symptoms from nicotine. By doing this I hope that you have had time to really understand why you smoke and can subsequently unravel the threads of your habit until it no longer exists.

Cutting Down?

Many of those who advise how to give up smoking advocate cutting down first to wean you off your habit slowly. Rather than going from smoking 25 a day to not smoking at all, they advise gradually cutting down from 25-20, then from 20-15, 15-10, 10-6 (the level at which you can cut down to without serious nicotine withdrawal – only low-level craving – in order to soften the blow).

This method can *only* work if you are incredibly strict with yourself. You will have to draw up a 'cutting down programme' and stick to it. It is all too easy to go out for the evening and think, 'oh, well it doesn't matter if I have those extra few' and before you know it you are back on 25 a day again. Only you know yourself well enough to know if this method will work for you. Unfortunately the great majority of us do not have the self-control to gradually reduce our nicotine intake over a period of time. If this is the case you will simply have to get it over and done with and go cold turkey.

Choosing A Day

Most people pick a day some time in the near future to give up. For a small minority of smokers, the thought that 'this is it!', will simply strike you as you are walking down the street and you will toss your packet of cigarettes in the bin and never smoke again. There is no right way of giving up, as it depends on the individual. Unfortunately, the latter scenario is somewhat rarer, so for those of you who know that you will never have that strength of commitment to simply give up on the spur of the moment, set a date, and stick to it!

There are two main types of day that people choose to give up smoking on:

1. High profile days which have little meaning to the individual, but act as a mass phenomenon, e.g. National No-Smoking Day, New Year's Day.

2. Days chosen by the individual prompted by their personal circumstances, i.e. pregnancy, illness, in preparation for an operation or simply because they feel that it is time to stop smoking.

Those who attempt to give up on the former, are unfortunately, more likely to fail. In the depressing aftermath of New Year numerous people break their resolutions, falling prey to chocolate, alcohol, or the dreaded tobacco before the month is out. This is mainly because these people did not have the personal motivation to give up, therefore easily wavered and returned to their habit.

On the contrary, those people who choose a day for a collection of personal reasons are giving up for *themselves* not because they feel that they ought to, therefore they are far more likely to succeed.

Setting A Date

Choose a suitable time in the foreseeable future when you will quit. It is best to plan a time when you don't have many social commitments. For example, prior to Christmas is almost certainly a recipe for disaster, whereas a quieter time of year when not much is going on is probably a better bet. By setting a 'suitable' date you are avoiding unnecessary temptation and making a difficult task somewhat simpler. However, having said this, I am *not* advocating that you spend *so* long pontificating over the perfect day to give up smoking, that you never actually get around to doing it!

Although smokers will always find reasons why this is definitely not a good time to give up, there are certainly times when it is easier to stop smoking. If you set a date and something major comes along and makes your life really difficult then it is a good idea to reconsider. For example if you have just lost your job or your partner, or your child is ill, you are not going to be in the right frame of mind to give up. There is really no point in making your 'quitting experience' more difficult than it will be anyway. If this does occur make sure that you keep your desire to give up smoking in mind and set a date when your life is more stable. To be quite honest if you have smoked for five or ten or even fifty years, another couple of weeks is not going to make a whole lot of difference (as long as it *is* only a matter of weeks!).

If you are feeling happy and confident you will be far more capable of coping with the problems that nicotine withdrawal throws your way and of overcoming them. If you stop smoking at the 'right' time as opposed to the 'wrong' time you are far less likely to start again. If you give up when you are not able to cope with other spheres of your life you will probably start again, feel dispirited and disheartened and put off trying again for even longer.

That Final Cigarette

Sorry – there is no easy way to get over this hurdle – you can't sneak around the issue you have to take the bull by its proverbial horns and smoke your last cigarette!

It is a good idea to mark the occasion by a ritualistic disposal of tobacco and tobacco-related paraphernalia. Collect together all of those matches, lighters, cigarette papers and emergency rations that are littered around your house, car or office and clutter up your bag. Empty all ashtrays, air your house and wash your clothes. This is all part of the cleansing process. If you have a partner that still smokes this is not going to be easy. If you can't persuade them to give up with you maybe you can ask them to restrict their smoking to certain rooms and forbid them to smoke in your car or bedroom.

Some people think that it is a good idea to keep a sealed packet of cigarettes in the house, because the temptation is sitting there, but you are able to resist it. However, if this seems akin to torture to you, get rid of everything. Everyone is different, and there is no *right* way to go about this – it is a means to an end. If you reach your goal of becoming a non-smoker, it doesn't matter how you got there (within reason and the law, obviously).

Day 1

You have probably prepared yourself for this day for some time now and it has now arrived, bringing a black cloud of dread and a feeling of horror that you ever thought that you could possibly give up smoking. However it is not all doom and gloom, you will probably also feel a certain amount of excitement and anticipation about the challenge of giving up. It is at that point that you need to find the list that you made back in Chapter 1 detailing the reasons why you are giving up. Read them and believe them.

Nicotine craving is always worst in the morning, because overnight your nicotine levels will have dropped right down. You may think that it would be obvious not to smoke at all on Day 1. On the contrary, I would suggest that you quickly smoke half a cigarette, stub it out and throw it away along with the rest of the packet. 'Why?' you ask. The answer is that this action actually serves two purposes:

1. If you are like me, you are probably not at your very best first thing in the morning, your head is fuzzy and your willpower is weak. If you try not to smoke at all you may find the combination of morning and giving up smoking too much. By smoking this half cigarette, you will temporarily

satisfy your nicotine craving and by the time your brain decides that it is ready for another dose of chemicals you will (hopefully) be in a better position to resist the urge.

2. It acts as a cut off point. By smoking your last cigarette the night before, as you do every day, and just getting up and not smoking, you have not decisively marked the event, even though you have made a conscious decision not to smoke. By smoking this half cigarette you are decisively stubbing it out and saying to yourself, 'that's it'. The action involved engraves the fact that you are quitting on your brain and you become aware that you have made a choice to give up smoking, it's not something that simply happened to you overnight.

The first few days of giving up smoking will be the hardest because you will have a strong desire to smoke coupled with changing routines that you may have adhered to for years. However, if you have read the preparation chapters carefully and refer to the checklist below, you will be in a position to get through the first few days without smoking.

You can have a cigarette

One of the major problems to accompany giving up smoking is a feeling of deprivation. This feeling that you are being denied something that you enjoy is very destructive to your attempt to give up smoking. By telling yourself you 'can't have a cigarette' or 'must not smoke' you begin a battle with yourself.

Unfortunately, such an internal conflict is very difficult to resolve and will probably conclude with you giving in and starting to smoke again. The way to avoid this situation, to prevent yourself feeling deprived – and probably eventually giving in to this self-imposed pressure – is to tell yourself that you *can* have a cigarette. This may seem contrary to logic, however as soon as you stop telling yourself that you cannot smoke and start telling yourself that you can smoke any time you please (you are simply choosing not to for the time being), you are giving yourself the element of choice.

By giving yourself this choice, giving up smoking is suddenly within your control. It becomes possible for you not to smoke without feeling deprived, cheated or dictated to. You are calling the shots. So, whenever you are craving nicotine, get through the craving in the ways that I have suggested, combined with the conscious thought that not smoking is *your* choice, and not something that has been imposed on you against your will and your better judgement.

How to get through the first few days without smoking:

- Avoid your usual routines and change your habits.
- Try to avoid smoking friends and going out in smoky environments.
- Try to avoid drinks that are high in caffeine (e.g. coffee).
- Nibble on healthy snacks.
- Keep a handy supply of sugar-free chewing gum.
- Brush your teeth frequently to remind yourself how nice it is to have fresh breath.
- Keep handy the list of reasons as to why you want to give up.
- Tell yourself you *can* smoke, you are simply not choosing to at present.
- Tell yourself that you won't be thinking about cigarettes the whole time, for the rest of your life, this is only a temporary stage.

- **Above all, keep busy. Do things that will take your mind off smoking.**

Week 1

Having got through the first day you should be feeling proud of yourself. See, you can do it, you can manage a whole day without nicotine and without your life falling apart. However, by this stage the withdrawal symptoms are probably starting to kick in and you may feel irritable, lethargic, develop a headache and begin to cough up the gunge that has been choking your lungs for so long.

Go with it. Every time you think, 'this isn't worth it, I feel worse', simply view it as a cleansing process. The nicotine devil that has been ruling your life is being deprived of the one thing needed to sustain itself. You may also experience moments of elation because you have taken control of your life at last.

Towards the end of Week 1, although you will undoubtedly have difficult times, you may be feeling that giving up smoking isn't so hard after all and you don't really know why you have been worrying, you could give up any time it doesn't have to be now. Don't be lulled into a false sense of security. Tell yourself that you don't want or need to smoke any more and keep at it.

How to get through the first week without smoking:

Keep following the advice for the 'first few days'. You will probably still need to avoid smoking friends and smoky environments (especially those group situations that involve alcohol in this first week), so make alternative arrangements:

- Ring up your non-smoking friends and suggest that you go for a quiet drink – this is a good way to break the alcohol/cigarette link in your mind.

- Go to the cinema.

- Stay in with a friend and watch a video.

- Go for a meal in a non-smoking restaurant.

- Curl up with a good book.

- Indulge yourself with a bubble bath and an early night.

- Do exercise/play sport.

By the end of the first week you will also start to *feel* the benefits of not smoking.

- Your sense of taste and smell will start to return. It may come as a shock to you that you have not been able to taste or smell properly for so long. Enjoy the 'new' smells and tastes that you experience.

- Your lungs will feel clearer and not so tight in the morning, although you will probably still be coughing, this will be a much 'looser' cough.

- You will feel calmer and more stable about life.

- You will feel confident that you have taken control of the situation.

- You will probably also experience feelings of elation that you can do this one thing that has been hanging over you for so long.

You will probably find that you still spend a lot of time thinking about cigarettes and smoking (remember, this won't go on forever). Don't try to avoid thinking about smoking. This is a sure-fire way to spend all day dreaming about cigarettes. Instead try and turn your thoughts into positive ones like 'I could have a cigarette right now, but I don't actually want one' or 'I would usually be smoking now, but I am quite content not to be smoking.' Try and 'float' above your cigarette cravings, go with your thoughts but *don't* let them get the better of you.

At this stage, one of the biggest worries for the smoker who is trying to give up, is that they will spend the rest of their lives thinking and dreaming about cigarettes and fighting off the cravings that accompany those thoughts. Fear not – you will not spend your life constantly thinking about cigarettes – over time these thoughts will become less and less frequent. You may still think about cigarettes now and again, but these will be passing thoughts rather than overpowering urges.

It is a good idea to give yourself little rewards, especially when you are feeling low about giving up smoking. Buy yourself something nice, treat yourself to a delicious supper or go and see that film that you have wanted to see for ages. After all, you deserve it.

The First Few Months

If you have got this far give yourself a pat on the back. However, don't become complacent. Just because you no longer think about smoking the whole time, this doesn't mean that you can have the odd one at a party simply because you are 'no longer addicted'. If you do this, the slippery slope to being a smoker again is not far away. Instead think 'I'm so glad I'm not wasting all that money on such a silly habit, and anyway if I've managed this long then I obviously need never smoke again.'

How not to ever smoke again:

- Tell yourself that you have got this far, so what is the point of going through all that again.

- Remain aware of the 'danger times'.

- Add up the savings that you are making from no longer being a smoker.

- Appreciate the fact that you have done something that you never thought you would be able to do and congratulate yourself.

- Recognise how much healthier and fitter you feel. Remember how much effort it took to run for the bus when you were a smoker.

- Appreciate how much more relaxed and confident you feel.

- Tell yourself that you will happy to never smoke another cigarette again for as long as you live – and mean it!

If at any point, in your new life as a non-smoker, you really feel the urge to smoke, re-examine the reasons that prompted you to give up in the first place and list the benefits that you have gained from not smoking. Ask yourself if you really want to go back to 'square one' all over again and to spend the next x months or years trying to attain the position that you are now in. If you have been truthful in your examination you will undoubtedly answer 'no' and put all thoughts of smoking again out of your mind.

9

What Happens If You Fail?

Even those who start off with the best intentions sometimes fall by the wayside. However, you have to look at it like a driving test or something similar – learn from your mistakes. What did you fail on last time? Where did the crosses (danger areas) appear? Learn from them, be aware of them and don't repeat them. Don't view it as a *failure* or a flaw in your character; look at it as a 'practice run'.

There are a number of reasons why people start smoking again, these include:

Scenario 1

You weaken and have a cigarette at a party under the influence of alcohol.

You probably won't enjoy it because you are no longer addicted to nicotine, so don't fall into the trap of thinking 'Oh, well I've had one cigarette, I might as well smoke a whole packet'. Instead think, 'I've made a mistake, but I can remedy it by not smoking any more.' The chances are that after only one cigarette you will not be re-addicted. Learn from your mistake and beware of this sort of situation in the future.

Scenario 2

Something bad happens in your life and you fall back on your old 'ally', tobacco.

You will probably smoke because you feel that you deserve it, because you have the excuse that something bad has happened and people will understand your failure. You will probably not enjoy smoking your first few cigarettes but put yourself through it nonetheless. As a result you will feel worse about yourself because not only is life treating you badly, but you are a failure because you have failed in your quest to give up smoking.

Never mind. When you have picked yourself up from life's blows, stop smoking again. It will not be as difficult this time because you have already broken the habit once and are secure in the knowledge that you are capable of doing it again. Tell yourself that this was simply a blip and that this time you will succeed.

Scenario 3

You become complacent and think that you can return to being a social smoker.

Wrong. Once you have been a smoker, you are far more likely to get re-addicted. You will start by pinching a fag off a friend at the end of an evening and progress to buying your own packet. You will then find that you have a few left over in the morning and think 'one cigarette won't do me any harm'. And before you can say 'twenty ******** lights please', you are a fully-fledged smoker again.

You have been warned about all of the above situations and now you know beyond doubt that they are danger spots. Don't be disheartened, the only way that you will succeed is to learn from your mistakes and never fall into the habit of thinking that you can have just one – no matter what the circumstances are.

Remember

- Use your failure as a practice run. Try again, you will be more determined not to fail again. Use the knowledge of what it was that let you down so that it doesn't happen again next time.

- One cigarette does not make you a smoker again. There is roughly a 50:50 chance of re-addiction. You will probably regret smoking one cigarette, so why do you need to go on and regret smoking a whole packet? Tell yourself, to err is human and don't smoke any more.

- Don't give up giving up. It's not easy. Don't be demoralised. It's not your fault, it is not because you are a weak person. But it will be if you don't attempt to beat it again.

- Remember, everyone can give up smoking, but like anything in life, some people will have more attempts before getting there than others.

- Don't sit back and say to yourself, 'It was fate, I obviously wasn't meant to give up – I was born to be a smoker.' This is rubbish and you know it. This is nicotine talking.

- Whatever you do, don't let nicotine get the better of you!

Conclusion

The high number of smokers in this country is living (and dying) proof of the difficulties attached to giving up smoking. I am not saying that giving up smoking is easy, however, if you are prepared to go a little way to understanding and unravelling your smoking habit, you are much closer to being able to give it up. When you actually understand that what it is you are leaving behind is not something that you can't live without and is something that you can't live long with, it will be much easier to let go.

Hopefully this book has gone some way towards allaying your fears concerning giving up smoking. Although making lists may all seem rather mundane at the time, believe me when you are desperate for a cigarette (and that little devil called nicotine almost has you in his grasp again), and you can pull out a list of the reasons that you wanted to give up in the first place, you will be in a much better position to put things in perspective. Hopefully, as a result, all those flimsy excuses that you were coming up with as to why you should smoke again will disappear in a puff of smoke – along with any desire you had to puff smoke.

Similarly, although 'danger times' may seem fairly obvious, if you haven't given them some prior consideration they will take you by surprise, and in your weakened state, you will not be in a position to make a rational decision and will automatically reach for tobacco to provide the answer. If you are aware of the problems you can circumnavigate them and prevent them ever occurring in the first place.

So, the key to giving up smoking is understanding your feelings surrounding smoking; laying your fears to rest and preparing yourself both physically and mentally. By doing this you are giving yourself an advantage, and anything that gives you an advantage over nicotine is a decisive step in the right direction.

I can almost guarantee that you will look back one day and realise that giving up smoking was one of the best decisions that you have ever made. Good luck.

Appendix

I know that I said that I wasn't going to bombard you with statistics. But, here are a few, just in case your resolve is weakening or even after reading this book you are still not sufficiently convinced to quit:

- About half of regular smokers will eventually die from smoking.

- Smoking causes 82% of all deaths from lung cancer, 83% of deaths from bronchitis and emphysema and around 25% of deaths from heart disease.

- One third of all cancer deaths can be attributed to smoking. These include:

  - lung cancer
  - mouth, lip and throat cancer
  - cancer of the pancreas
  - bladder cancer
  - cancer of the kidney
  - stomach cancer
  - liver cancer
  - leukaemia

- People who smoke 1-15 cigarettes are eight times more likely to die of lung cancer than non-smokers.

- People who smoke 25+ cigarettes a day are 25 times more likely to die of lung cancer than non-smokers.

- Female smokers who take the contraceptive pill are 10 times more likely to suffer from a stroke, heart attack or cardiovascular disease than non-smokers who use the pill.

- Smoking has been associated with impotence and sperm abnormalities in men.

- In pregnant women, smoking leads to an increased risk of:

    −spontaneous abortion
    −haemorrhaging
    −premature birth
    −low weight of babies at birth, which can lead to a greater risk of ill-health
    −Sudden Infant Death Syndrome

- More than 17,000 children under 5 are admitted to hospital every year due to the effects of passive smoking.

- 120,000 smokers in the UK die from smoking every year.

- The UK government earned almost £10.5 million from tobacco duty and VAT in 1997.

- The government spends under £10 million a year on health campaigns against tobacco use.

Other books in the Help! series:

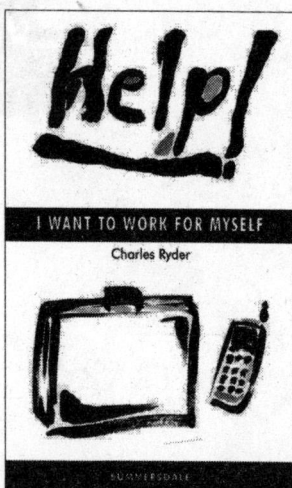

Help!

I DON'T UNDERSTAND COMPUTERS

Paul Bassett

SUMMERSDALE

Help!

I WANT TO GET FIT

Katy Bircher & Katie Goodwin

SUMMERSDALE

Help!

I'M BUYING A HOUSE

Alastair Williams

SUMMERSDALE

Help!

I WANT TO WORK FOR MYSELF

Charles Ryder

SUMMERSDALE